DISCOVERING MATH

DIVISION

DAVID L. STIENECKER

ART BY RICHARD MACCABE

BENCHMARK BOOKS

MARSHALL CAVENDISH
NEW YORK

Benchmark Books
Marshall Cavendish Corporation
99 White Plains Road
Tarrytown, New York 10591-9001

©Marshall Cavendish Corporation, 1996

Series created by Blackbirch Graphics, Inc.

Printed and bound in the United States.

Library of Congress Cataloging-in-Publication Data

Stienecker, David.
    Division / by David Stienecker.
        p.   cm. — (Discovering math)
    Includes index.
    ISBN 0-7614-0596-8 (lib. bdg.)
    1. Division—Juvenile literature. 2. Mathematical recreations—Juvenile literature. [1. Division. 2. Mathematical recreations.] I. Title. II. Series.
QA115.S784   1995
513.2'14—dc20

95-13577
CIP
AC

Contents

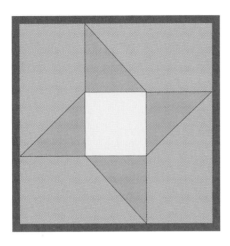

The Friendship Star

Ever heard of a friendship star? This is what it looks like. The pattern is made from triangles.

- How many triangles are used to make the star?

- How many stars could you make with fifteen triangles? Would you have any triangles left over? How could you find out?

- To check your answer, make fifteen triangles like this one. Use them to make friendship stars.

If you know how many in each group, you can divide to find how many groups.

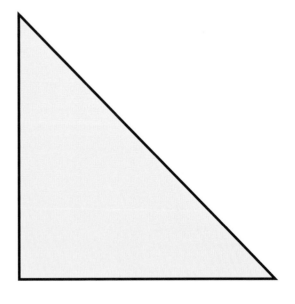

Friendship stars are used as a pattern in some patchwork quilts. Patchwork quilts are a kind of blanket. They are made by sewing small pieces of cloth together. That's why they are called "patchwork."

Here is what a patchwork quilt made with friend-ship stars might look like.

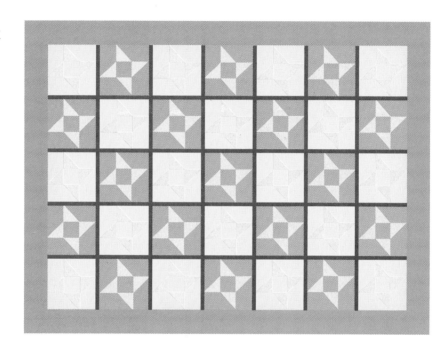

• There are 140 triangles in this quilt. How many friendship stars were made from the triangles? Use a division problem to find the answer.

• Now suppose you want to use a star like this one to make a quilt. If you have 140 triangles, how many stars like this can you make? Will there by any triangles left over?

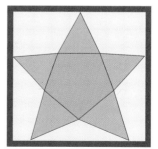

Facts Five

This game is played just like bingo. Any number of people can play. One person will have to be chosen as the caller. He or she should know division facts.

Each player will need:

25 playing pieces or "markers"

paper and pencil

Have each player draw a game board like this one on a sheet of paper.

F	A	C	T	S

Then each player writes a number from 1 through 9 in each of the boxes on his or her game board, like this:

F	A	C	T	S
3	7	4	3	6
5	8	4	2	9
9	7	1	4	3
6	4	5	1	2
8	3	4	9	3

How to play:

• The caller calls out a question on division facts. For example, "Under A, how many 4's in 20," or "Under S, what is 12 divided by 3." The caller should write down all of the calls he or she makes.

• The players who have the number that solves the division fact should cover the number with a marker.

• The first player to completely cover all the numbers in a row, column, or diagonal calls out "Facts" and wins the game.

• The leader uses his or her record of calls to check the winner's card.

• For a new game, use the same card, make new ones, or exchange cards.

7

Dividing by Subtracting

Division is just another way of subtracting the same number over and over again. You can see how this works by using a calculator.

To find 30 ÷ 6, count how many 6's can be subtracted from 30, like this:

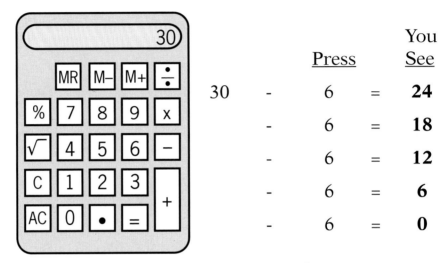

		Press	You See
30	-	6 =	**24**
	-	6 =	**18**
	-	6 =	**12**
	-	6 =	**6**
	-	6 =	**0**

• How many 6's were subtracted from 30?

• Use a calculator to do a little division by subtraction. Try it with these division problems. Some of them will have remainders. When you are finished, try some problems of your own.

36 ÷ 6	49 ÷ 7	28 ÷ 4	27 ÷ 3	64 ÷ 8
45 ÷ 5	36 ÷ 9	46 ÷ 7	54 ÷ 6	72 ÷ 9
36 ÷ 4	49 ÷ 8	35 ÷ 5	63 ÷ 9	58 ÷ 7
75 ÷ 6	95 ÷ 5	37 ÷ 4	57 ÷ 9	49 ÷ 5

Dividing by 9's and 3's

It's easy to tell if a number can be evenly divided by 9. All you have to do is add the number's digits. If the sum is more than one digit, add up the digits again.

Continue in this way until you have only one digit left. If the digit is 9, then the original number is divisible by 9. Here's an example:

- Can 468 be evenly divided by 9?

  Add the digits. $4 + 6 + 8 = 18$

  Add again. $1 + 8 = 9$

  The single-digit sum is 9. So 468 is divisible by 9.

You can use the same method to find out if a number can be exactly divided by 3. If the single-digit sum is 3, 6, or 9, then the original number is divisible by 3.

- Can 348 be evenly divided by 3?

  Add the digits. $3 + 4 + 8 = 15$

  Add again. $1 + 5 = 6$

  The single-digit is 6. So 348 is divisible by 3.

- Use this method to find out which of these numbers can be evenly divided by 3 and 9.

  765   267   376   558   2,126   1,362   4,063

  1,125   11,574   59,239   2,886   22,359

Beanstalk Race

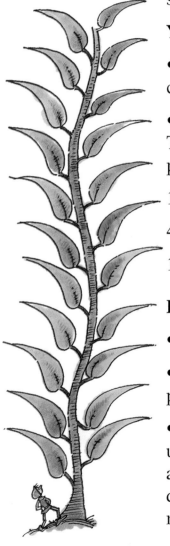

Have you ever heard the story of Jack and the beanstalk? Jack climbs a really tall beanstalk to look for a goose that lays golden eggs. But when he gets to the top he runs into a giant and barely escapes with his skin.

Here's a beanstalk game to play. The object is to see who can get to the top-most leaf first.

You will need:

• Two different markers. You might use two coins or buttons, but anything small will do.

• Paper and pencil and a deck of division cards. To make the deck, write each of these division problems on an index card.

$14 \div 7$	$20 \div 5$	$36 \div 6$	$16 \div 2$	$55 \div 9$	$24 \div 7$
$43 \div 6$	$64 \div 9$	$74 \div 8$	$83 \div 9$	$33 \div 4$	$50 \div 8$
$14 \div 3$	$27 \div 8$	$48 \div 9$	$59 \div 7$	$19 \div 4$	$20 \div 3$

How to play:

• Turn the cards face down and mix them up.

• Each player draws a card in turn, solves the problem, and returns the card to the pile.

• If the division problem has a remainder, move up that number of leaves. Land on the same leaf as your opponent, and he or she must move down two leaves. If you solve a problem with no remainder, move down two leaves.

Cross Numbers

This game is like a crossword puzzle except with numbers. The clues are division problems. The answers are the quotients.

Copy or trace the cross numbers puzzle onto a sheet of paper. Then give it a try.

The answer to a division problem is called a quotient.

Across

(2) $2\overline{)66}$

(4) $4\overline{)604}$

(7) $6\overline{)192}$

(9) $3\overline{)171}$

(11) $12\overline{)300}$

(12) $10\overline{)910}$

(14) $12\overline{)504}$

(16) $8\overline{)608}$

(18) $3\overline{)258}$

(20) $15\overline{)345}$

(22) $21\overline{)252}$

(24) $7\overline{)574}$

(25) $9\overline{)747}$

(27) $11\overline{)352}$

(29) $6\overline{)792}$

1.		2.	3.		4.	5.	6.
7.	8.		9.	10.		11.	
	12.	13.		14.	15.		
		16.	17.		18.	19.	
20.	21.		22.	23.		24.	
	25.	26.		27.	28.		
					29.		

Down

(1) $4\overline{)92}$

(3) $5\overline{)175}$

(5) $3\overline{)156}$

(6) $12\overline{)180}$

(8) $10\overline{)290}$

(10) $13\overline{)962}$

(13) $8\overline{)136}$

(15) $30\overline{)840}$

(17) $13\overline{)793}$

(19) $9\overline{)612}$

(21) $22\overline{)836}$

(23) $42\overline{)966}$

(26) $21\overline{)672}$

(28) $19\overline{)399}$

11

Remainder Riddle

Most of the problems in this table are simple division facts. But some have remainders. Make a copy of the table. Shade in all the boxes with remainders and you'll have the answer to this riddle:

How can you spell mousetrap with three letters?

3 ÷ 2	5 ÷ 2	7 ÷ 2	8 ÷ 2	11 ÷ 2	13 ÷ 2	15 ÷ 2
17 ÷ 2	18 ÷ 2	3 ÷ 3	6 ÷ 3	11 ÷ 3	12 ÷ 3	17 ÷ 3
19 ÷ 3	21 ÷ 3	24 ÷ 3	27 ÷ 3	6 ÷ 4	9 ÷ 4	14 ÷ 4
18 ÷ 4	20 ÷ 4	24 ÷ 4	28 ÷ 4	33 ÷ 4	36 ÷ 4	7 ÷ 5
13 ÷ 5	16 ÷ 5	22 ÷ 5	25 ÷ 5	31 ÷ 5	35 ÷ 5	42 ÷ 5
45 ÷ 5	6 ÷ 6	15 ÷ 6	19 ÷ 6	28 ÷ 6	30 ÷ 6	36 ÷ 6
42 ÷ 6	48 ÷ 6	56 ÷ 6	9 ÷ 7	17 ÷ 7	21 ÷ 7	28 ÷ 7
35 ÷ 7	42 ÷ 7	49 ÷ 7	59 ÷ 7	63 ÷ 7	8 ÷ 8	16 ÷ 8
24 ÷ 8	32 ÷ 8	40 ÷ 8	49 ÷ 8	56 ÷ 8	64 ÷ 8	72 ÷ 8
18 ÷ 9	27 ÷ 9	36 ÷ 9	57 ÷ 9	63 ÷ 9	72 ÷ 9	81 ÷ 9

- Now that you know the answer to the riddle, try making some remainder riddle puzzles of your own. Give them to friends to solve.

Mystery Square

The mystery square below holds an interesting secret. To unlock the secret, you'll need to do a little division.

First trace or make a copy of the mystery square. You can leave out the division problems.

12)52	10)69	17)53
19)79	13)96	15)157
18)116	22)441	11)358

Now solve the division problems in each box. Each one will have a remainder. Write the remainder in its box in your mystery square.

When your mystery square is finished, add up each row, column, and diagonal. The secret is in the sums. Did you discover it?

Greatest Quotient Game

Here's a division game you can play with any number of people. These are the things you will need:

a deck of playing cards

paper and pencil for each player

Before playing, prepare the deck of cards by taking out all the face cards and ten cards. Let the aces stand for 1's and the jokers stand for 0's.

Have each player draw a game board like this one on a sheet of paper.

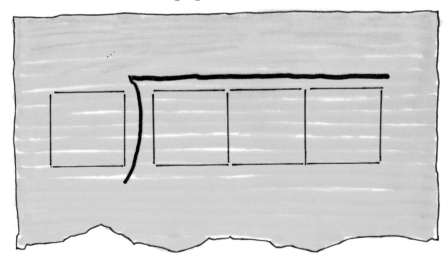

How to play:

1. Shuffle the cards and lay them face down.

2. In turn, each player takes a card and reads the number aloud. Remember aces are 1's and jokers are 0's.

3. Each player writes the number in any of the boxes on his or her game board. Here's what one player's game board might look like after a 3 and an 8 card have been drawn.

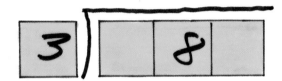

4. After four cards have been drawn, each player's board will have a one-digit divisor and a three-digit dividend. This is how a game board might look at this stage of the game.

5. Each player should solve his or her division problem. The winner is the one with the greatest quotient. What is the quotient of the above game board?

• Try this twist on the game. After everyone has solved their problems, give them 60 seconds to rearrange their digits to try and make a larger quotient. What's the secret?

• Here's another way to play the game. Have players add another digit to the divisor. Or, have them add another digit to the dividend. Draw five cards instead of four.

The Path of No Remainders

It's easy to get through this maze if you know how to divide. Just solve the problems and follow the path of no remainders. Try using mental math and see how fast it goes!

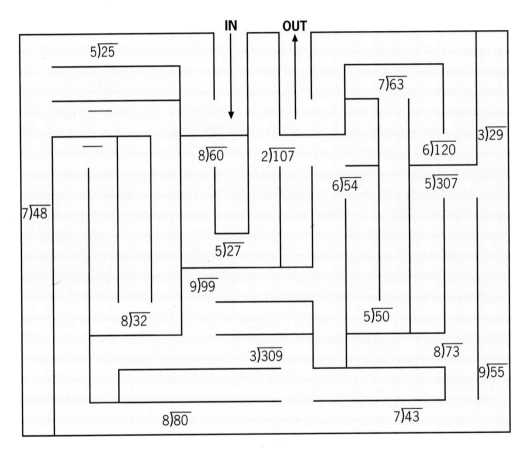

Make a division maze of your own. Show the way out with problems that have no remainders. Or, do it the other way around. Give your maze to a friend. See how quickly your friend can divide.

Missing Numbers Puzzles

Here are some puzzles that will test your thinking skills. Solve them by yourself or with the help of a clever friend.

Try to figure out the missing numbers in these division problems. These will get you started.

It's not as hard as it looks!

```
      2?              ??              1?              1?
  ? )9?          3 )8?          6 )??          ? )?1
    8               6               ?               7
   16              ??              24              ??
   ??              ?7              ??              2?
    0               0               0               0
```

These are a little bit tougher.

```
      3?             1??             ???
  ??)? ??         ? )?8?         7 )???
    36               5               7
    38              18              25
    ??              ??              ??
     ?              35              ??
                    ??              49
                     ?               ?
```

• Try making up some missing number puzzles of your own. Making them is as much of a challenge as solving them.

17

Pyramid Puzzles

Here are some pyramid puzzles to warm up your division know-how. Here's the key to the puzzles:

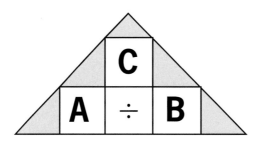

$$A \div B = C$$

Here's an example:

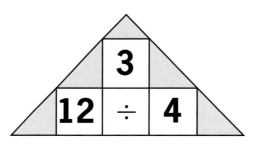

Here are a couple of simple puzzles to get you started.

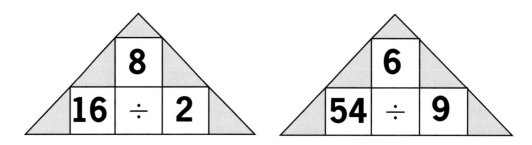

These puzzles are a little bit harder. Remember the pyramid pattern as you solve them. Refer to the key if you get confused.

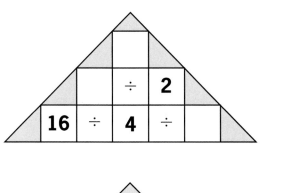

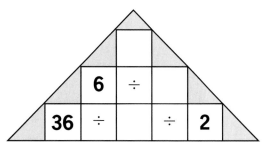

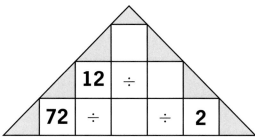

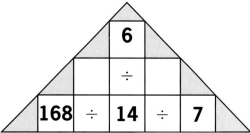

This one will really tug at your brain. Give it a try!

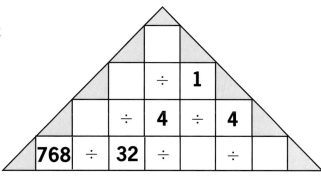

Making the pyramid puzzles is as much of a puzzle as the puzzles themselves. Try making a few and giving them to friends to solve.

A Visit to an Enchanted Forest

Play this game with a friend and work your way through the enchanted forest. Use a penny and a dime for markers. Throw a die (one of a pair of dice) to tell how many spaces to move. Or, make six number cards. Draw and replace a card during each turn. Always mix the cards up between turns.

How to play:

1. The first player throws the die, then moves that number of spaces. You should count the "Start" square.

2. Land on a blue sum square and you don't have to do anything until your next turn. If you land on a division problem square, find the quotient and move your marker to the square where the quotient appears. If you land on a square with words, do what it says.

3. Watch for those short cuts and danger zones! They can make life really easy or really difficult.

4. The first person to get to the end wins!

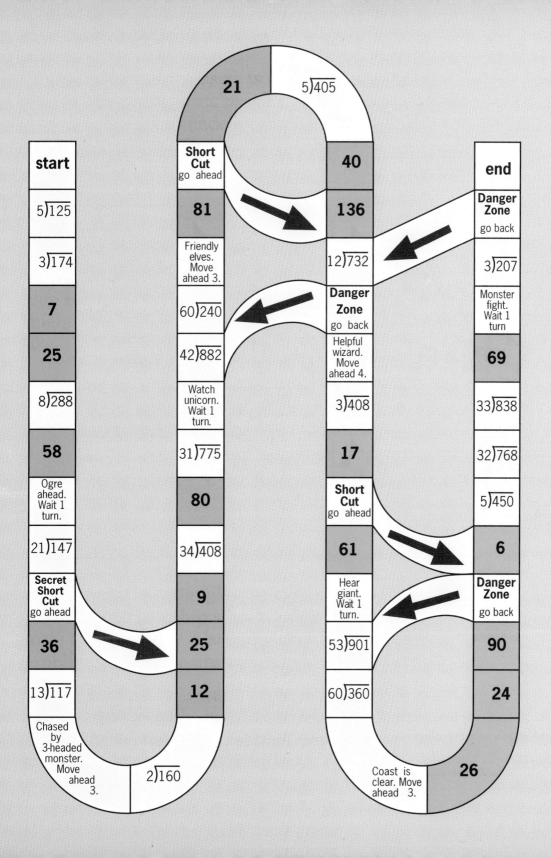

Division Decoder

Use the decoder to find the answers to the riddles below. To decode the decoder just find the quotient for each letter of the alphabet. (Hint: Each quotient has a remainder.)

DECODER						
A	**B**	**C**	**D**	**E**	**F**	**G**
4)81	18)39	27)60	53)63	35)74	16)98	17)71
H	**I**	**J**	**K**	**L**	**M**	**N**
31)95	27)59	2)163	7)219	3)158	5)459	9)818
O	**P**	**Q**	**R**	**S**	**T**	**U**
4)133	6)435	8)413	5)376	7)508	18)205	12)257
V	**W**	**X**	**Y**	**Z**		
13)135	27)604	12)379	13)125	24)362		

What is hard to beat?

20RI   3 R2•20 R1•75 R1•1 R10

2 R3•33 R1•2 R5•52 R2•2 R4•1 R10

2 R4•4 R3•4R3

What kind of insect goes skin diving?

20 R1   81 R4•33 R1•72R5•51 R5•21 R5•

2 R5•11 R7•33 RI

What animal keeps the best time?

20 R1   22 R10•20 R1•11 R7•2 R6•3 R2•
1 R10•33 R1•4 R3

How can a piece of wood become a king?

2 R3•9 R8   2 R3•2 R4•2 R5•90 R8•4 R3
81 R4•20 R1•1 R10•2 R4   2 R5•90 R8•11 R7•33 R1
20 R1   75 R1•21 R5•52 R2•2 R4•75 R1

How can you fall off a ladder without getting hurt?

6 R2•20 R1•52 R2•52 R2   6 R2•75 R1•33 R1•81R4
11 R7•3 R2•2 R4   2 R3•33 R1•11 R7•11 R7•
33 R1•81 R4   75 R1•21 R5•90 R8•4 R3

What happens when a cat eats a lemon?

2 R5•11 R7   2 R3•2 R4•2 R6•33 R1•81 R4•
2 R4•72 R5   20 R1   72 R5•33 R1•21 R5•75 R1
72 R3•21 R5•72 R5•72 R5

• Use the decoder to write some riddles of your own. Better yet, have fun and make up your own division code.

Dividing with Mayan Numbers

The Maya are an Indian people who have lived in Central America for over 1,700 years. They developed a system of numbers based on only three symbols—a dot, a dash, and an oval.

• Solve each of the division problems below. Use the chart to decode the Mayan numbers. Write your answers in Mayan symbols.

Our System	Mayan System
1	•
2	••
3	•••
4	••••
5	——
6	• / ——
7	•• / ——
8	••• / ——
9	•••• / ——
10	═
11	• / ═
12	•• / ═
13	••• / ═
14	•••• / ═
15	≡
16	• / ≡
17	•• / ≡
18	••• / ≡
19	•••• / ≡
20	⬯
40	⬯⬯
60	••• / ⬯

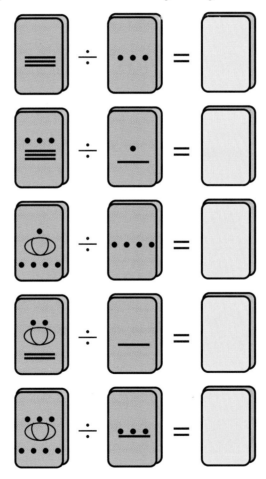

• Use Mayan numbers to make some division problems of your own.

More Riddles and Games

Here are a few more riddles and puzzles to razzle and dazzle you. They all have something to do with division. Give them a try. When you're finished, pass them on to a friend.

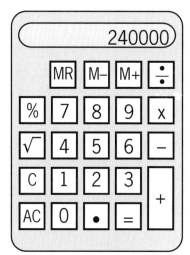

Guess the number of zeros in each quotient. Then divide with a calculator to check your guess.

180 ÷ 30   800 ÷ 20
2,800 ÷ 40   6,000 ÷ 50   9,000 ÷ 30
800 ÷ 400   16,000 ÷ 800
40,000 ÷ 80   240,000 ÷ 60

Here are two more puzzles to solve:

The makers of Crunch Chips had a special offer. Collect 8 labels and get 1 bag free.

Kim persuaded all her friends to give their labels to her. She collected 71 labels in all. How many free bags of Crunch Chips was Kim able to get?

Two mothers and 2 daughters divided 3 oranges among themselves. Each person received 1 whole orange. How could this be possible?

25

Three-Digit Number Puzzle

Select any three-digit number and repeat it to make a six-digit number—for example: 123123. These four things will always be true:

1. Your six-digit number can be equally divided by 13. **123123 ÷ 13 = 9471**

2. The quotient you get when you divide by 13 can be equally divided by 11.
9471 ÷ 11 = 861

3. The quotient you get after dividing by 11 can be equally divided by 7. **861 ÷ 7 = 123**

4. The quotient you get after you divide by 7 is your original three-digit number. **123**

Test it out with a calculator. Then show it to some friends. They will be amazed.

Honey Pots

Joe Bear has 21 honey pots. Seven pots are full of honey and 7 contain no honey at all. Three are half-full and 4 are half-empty.

Joe wants to divide his honey pots with his sister and brother. Each bear will receive the same number of pots and an equal amount of honey.

No honey will be poured from one pot to another. None of the bears will have 4 pots of the same kind—full, half-full, half-empty, or empty. How does Joe divide his honey pots? (Hint: It helps to draw a picture.)

Answers

Pps. 4–5, The Friendship Star

Since each friendship star uses 4 triangles, you need to find how many groups of 4 are in 15. You can use a division problem to find the answer:

```
      3 R 3
  4) 1 5
   - 1 2
       3
```

You can make 3 stars and have 3 triangles left over.

You can find how many friendship stars are in the quilt by dividing to find how many groups of 4 are in 140.

```
        3 5
  4) 1 4 0
   - 1 2
       2 0
     - 2 0
       0 0
```

The 5-pointed star takes 5 triangles to make. Use a division problem to find out how many groups of 5 are in 140.

There are 28 with no triangles left over.

```
          2 8
  5) 1 4 0
   - 1 0
       4 0
     - 4 0
       0 0
```

Pps. 6-7, Facts Five

No answers.

P. 8, Dividing by Subtracting

Five 6's were subtracted from 30.

$36 \div 6 = 6$	$49 \div 7 = 7$	$28 \div 4 = 7$
$45 \div 5 = 9$	$36 \div 9 = 4$	$46 \div 7 = 6R4$
$36 \div 4 = 9$	$49 \div 8 = 6R1$	$35 \div 5 = 7$
$75 \div 6 = 12R3$	$95 \div 5 = 19$	$37 \div 4 = 9R1$

$27 \div 3 = 9$	$64 \div 8 = 8$
$54 \div 6 = 9$	$72 \div 9 = 8$
$63 \div 9 = 7$	$58 \div 7 = 8R2$
$57 \div 9 = 6R3$	$49 \div 5 = 9R4$

P. 9, Dividing by 9's and 3's

765 (9,3)   267 (3)   376 (neither)
558 (9,3)   2,126 (neither)   1,362 (3)
4,063 (neither)   1,125 (9,3)
11,574 (9,3)   59,239 (neither)
2,886 (3)   22,359 (3)

27

Answers

P. 10, Beanstalk Race

$14 \div 7 = 2$ $20 \div 5 = 4$

$43 \div 6 = 7R1$ $64 \div 9 = 7R1$

$14 \div 3 = 4R2$ $27 \div 8 = 3R3$

$36 \div 6 = 6$ $16 \div 2 = 8$

$74 \div 8 = 9R2$ $83 \div 9 = 8R2$

$48 \div 9 = 5R3$ $59 \div 7 = 8R3$

$55 \div 9 = 6R1$ $24 \div 7 = 3R3$

$33 \div 4 = 8R1$ $50 \div 8 = 6R2$

$19 \div 4 = 4R3$ $20 \div 3 = 6R2$

P. 11, Cross Numbers

1.2		2.3	3.3		4.1	5.5	6.1
7.3	8.2		9.5	10.7		11.2	5
	12.9	13.1		14.4	15.2		
		16.7	17.6		18.8	19.6	
20.2	21.3		22.1	2		24.8	2
	25.8	26.3		27.3	28.2		
		2			29.1	3	2

P. 12, Remainder Riddle

$3 \div 2$	$5 \div 2$	$7 \div 2$	$8 \div 2$	$11 \div 2$	$13 \div 2$	$15 \div 2$
$17 \div 2$	$18 \div 2$	$3 \div 3$	$6 \div 3$	$11 \div 3$	$12 \div 3$	$17 \div 3$
$19 \div 3$	$21 \div 3$	$24 \div 3$	$27 \div 3$	$6 \div 4$	$9 \div 4$	$14 \div 4$
$18 \div 4$	$20 \div 4$	$24 \div 4$	$28 \div 4$	$33 \div 4$	$36 \div 4$	$7 \div 5$
$13 \div 5$	$16 \div 5$	$22 \div 5$	$25 \div 5$	$31 \div 5$	$35 \div 5$	$42 \div 5$
$45 \div 5$	$6 \div 6$	$15 \div 6$	$19 \div 6$	$28 \div 6$	$30 \div 6$	$36 \div 6$
$42 \div 6$	$48 \div 6$	$56 \div 6$	$9 \div 7$	$17 \div 7$	$21 \div 7$	$28 \div 7$
$35 \div 7$	$42 \div 7$	$49 \div 7$	$59 \div 7$	$63 \div 7$	$8 \div 8$	$16 \div 8$
$24 \div 8$	$32 \div 8$	$40 \div 8$	$49 \div 8$	$56 \div 8$	$64 \div 8$	$72 \div 8$
$18 \div 9$	$27 \div 9$	$36 \div 9$	$57 \div 9$	$63 \div 9$	$72 \div 9$	$81 \div 9$

P. 13, Mystery Square

This is what your mystery square should look like when it's finished:

4	9	2
3	5	7
8	1	6

The secret is that the sum of each row, column, and diagonal is equal to 15. Here are the answers to the division problems:

$12 \overline{)52}$ 4 R4 $10 \overline{)69}$ 6 R9 $17 \overline{)53}$ 3 R2

$19 \overline{)79}$ 4 R3 $13 \overline{)96}$ 7 R5 $15 \overline{)157}$ 10 R7

$18 \overline{)116}$ 6 R8 $22 \overline{)441}$ 20 R1 $11 \overline{)358}$ 32 R6

Pps. 14–15, Greatest Quotient Game

The answer to the division problem on the game board is 62.

The secret to getting a larger quotient is to make the divisor smaller or the dividend larger.

P. 16, The Path of No Remainders

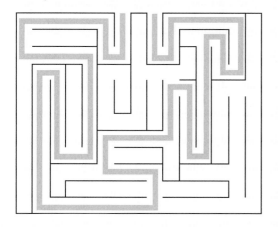

P. 17, Missing Numbers Puzzles

```
    2 4          2 9          1 4          1 3
4) 9 6       3) 8 7       6) 8 4       7) 9 1
   8            6            6            7
  ---          ---          ---          ---
  1 6          2 7          2 4          2 1
  1 6          2 7          2 4          2 1
  ---          ---          ---          ---
    0            0            0            0
```

```
      3 3            1 3 7          1 3 7
12) 3 9 8       5) 6 8 5       7) 9 5 9
    3 6            5              7
    ---            ---            ---
    3 8            1 8            2 5
    3 6            1 5            2 1
    ---            ---            ---
      2            3 5            4 9
                   3 5            4 9
                   ---            ---
                     0              0
```

Pps. 18–19, Pyramid Puzzles

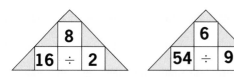

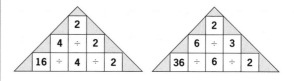

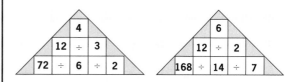

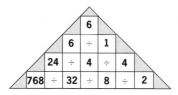

Pps. 20–21, A Visit to an Enchanted Forest

No answers.

Pps. 22–23, Division Decoder

DECODER						
A	**B**	**C**	**D**	**E**	**F**	**G**
20 R1	2 R3	2 R6	1 R10	2 R4	6 R2	4 R3
H	**I**	**J**	**K**	**L**	**M**	**N**
3 R2	2 R5	81 R1	31 R2	52 R2	81 R4	90 R8
O	**P**	**Q**	**R**	**S**	**T**	**U**
33 R1	72 R3	51 R5	75 R1	72 R5	11 R7	21 R5
V	**W**	**X**	**Y**	**Z**		
10 R5	22 R10	32 R7	9 R8	15 R2		

Answers

What is hard to beat?
A hard-boiled egg.

What kind of insect goes skin diving?
A mosquito.

What animal keeps the best time?
A watchdog.

How can a piece of wood become a king?
By being made into a ruler.

How can you fall off a ladder without getting hurt?
Fall from the bottom rung.

What happens when a cat eats a lemon?
It becomes a sour puss.

P. 24, Dividing by Mayan Numbers
$15 \div 3 =$ — $50 \div 5 =$ ═

$18 \div 6 =$ • • • $64 \div 8 =$ •••

$24 \div 4 =$ •

P. 25, More Riddles and Games
$180 \div 30 = 6$ (no zeros); $800 \div 20 = 40$ (one zero); $2,800 \div 40 = 70$ (one zero); $6,000 \div 50 = 120$ (one zero); $9,000 \div 30 = 300$ (two zeros); $800 \div 400 = 2$ (no zeros); $16,000 \div 800 = 20$ (one zero); $40,000 \div 80 = 500$ (two zeros); $240,000 \div 60 = 4,000$ (three zeros)

Kim will get 10 free bags in all. This is how. She will get 8 free bags with the 71 labels and have 7 labels left over. Each of the 8 free bags has a label so she uses them to get her ninth free bag. With the ninth bag's labels and the 7 labels she had left over at the beginning, Kim can get her tenth bag.

Each person received 1 orange because one of the mothers is also a daughter. So, there is a total of three people.

P. 26, Three-Digit Number Puzzle.
No answers.

P. 26, Honey Pots:

	Full	Half-Full	Empty	Half-Empty
Joe	3	0	3	1
brother	2	3	2	0
sister	2	0	2	3

Glossary

column An up-and-down arrangement of things.

diagonal A line connecting opposite corners of a shape.

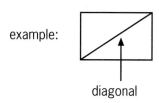

example:

diagonal

digits The symbols used to write numerals: 0, 1, 2, 3, 4, 5, 6, 7, 8, and 9.

dividend The number that is divided in a division problem.

$$\overset{4}{6\overline{)24}} \longrightarrow \text{dividend}$$

division A mathematical operation with two numbers that results in a quotient.

divisor The number by which a dividend is divided.

$$\text{divisor} \longrightarrow \overset{4}{6\overline{)24}}$$

quotient The answer to a division problem (other than the remainder).

$$\overset{4 \longrightarrow \text{quotient}}{6\overline{)27}} \\ \underline{-24} \\ 3$$

remainder The number left over in a division problem. The remainder must be less than the divisor.

$$\overset{4}{6\overline{)27}} \\ \underline{-24} \\ 3 \longrightarrow \text{remainder}$$

row A number of objects arranged in a straight line.

sum The number obtained by adding two or more numbers together.

triangle A shape with three sides.

Index